My Military Story
Bucket Journal

Document Your Service,
Share Your Memories, and
Create a Legacy For Future Generations

"Start a conversation with us. Ask us how we are, if we need help, if there is something you could do to help us in that moment. You can even ask us what happened. Don't ask us if we killed someone, but maybe ask if we have a story to share. A lot of us want to share what happened, but we just don't know how."

©2021 by My Bucket Journals LLC
Hutto, Texas 78634

Designed and printed in the USA. All rights reserved.

This publication may not be reproduced stored or transmitted in whole or in part, in any form or by any means, electronic, mechanical or otherwise, without prior written consent from the publisher and author.

Brief quotations may be included in a review. If in PDF form, it may be stored on your computer and you may keep one online digital copy. This publication may be printed for personal use only.

Disclaimer
The information in this book is based on the author's opinion, knowledge and experience. The publisher and the author will not be held liable for the use or misuse of the information contained herein.

Disclosure
This book may contain affiliate links. If you click through an affiliate link to a third-party website and make a purchase, the author may receive a small commission.

Cover photo ©DepositPhotos

This journal is adapted from the book "Served With Pride" by Claudia Bartow ©2013. Thank you, Claudia, for your tireless support of America's veterans. Used with permission.

We Believe in Supporting Veterans

...and so do you! *For every My Military Story Bucket Journal sold*, My Bucket Journals will donate $2 to one of the following organizations.

National Honor Flight Network https://www.honorflight.org/
The mission of Honor Flight is to transport America's veterans to Washington, D.C. to visit the memorials dedicated to honoring those who have served and sacrificed for our country. Participation in an Honor Flight trip gives veterans the opportunity to share this momentous occasion with other comrades, to remember friends and comrades lost, and share their stories and experiences with other veterans. All honored veterans travel at no cost to the veteran.

Homes for Our Troops https://www.hfotusa.org/
This organization builds and donates specially adapted custom homes nationwide for severely injured post-9/11 Veterans, to enable them to rebuild their lives. Most of these Veterans have sustained injuries including multiple limb amputations, partial or full paralysis, and/or severe traumatic brain injury (TBI). These homes restore some of the freedom and independence our Veterans sacrificed while defending our country, and enable them to focus on their family, recovery, and rebuilding their lives.

Wounded Warrior Project https://www.woundedwarriorproject.org/
Every warrior has unique challenges and goals. That's why Wounded Warrior Project provides a variety of veteran programs and services to help service members take the steps that are right for them. With the tremendous support of donors, veterans never pay a penny to get the help they need to build the future they deserve. Their comprehensive programs include mental wellness, physical wellness, career and VA benefits counseling, and a veterans crisis hotline.

Introduction

Congratulations!

You have taken the first step to recording the details, stories and memories of your military service. This journal will give you all the tools you need to reflect, record, and preserve your history.

Throughout history, stories have been passed down from generation to generation. They are the fabric of our lives and help us understand who we are and where we came from. If you served in the military you have stories to tell, probably many of them, and there are people all around you who are ready to hear your tales.

Every military veteran is a hero with stories to tell. Some are funny, some are sad, but mostly they have an important place in history that helps us understand the sacrifices made for our freedom. These stories also give us a peak into the powerful impact of military service on one's life. You might be very surprised how much your family, friends, and community will enjoy your insight into this time of your life!

You should be proud of your service, whether you served during wartime, or peacetime, were an infantryman or cook. With this journal you have room to record the memories and make sure your service is not forgotten.

The next few pages will tell you exactly how to use it. As you will see, you can customize it easily to work for you. Once you begin the journey of telling your military story you may even be interested in using one of the sharing methods discussed later in this journal.

If you find it difficult to talk about these things on your own, ask family members to participate. We hope you can use this journal as a tool to draw family closer together and as a means of promoting better understanding.

Thank you for your service and for sharing your story.

You Can Easily Customize This Guide

No two people who served in the military have the exact same experience. Some were in the Navy and served on boats. Some served in combat or in foreign lands, while others served stateside. Some were assigned to multiple posts, deployments or units.

This journal was made to work for you no matter what your history.

If you see a place for reflection that does not describe you, that you did not experience, or are not ready to share about, simply skip the section and move on to the next one.

Perhaps you served on six different ships, but there is only room for recording your memories of three? Feel free to copy those blank pages, fill in the information and slip them into this journal as needed.

Did you serve in the Air Force and the Army? Copy the pages needed and insert them one after the other.

While every effort was made to allow for as many unique situations as possible, you can easily adapt what is provided to make it the perfect collection for your story.

Table of Contents

- Basic Information About Me – 7
- Military Promotions - 8
- My Medals - 9
- Other Recognitions - 12
- Military Friends - 13
- Enlistment or being drafted - 14
- Basic Training/Boot Camp/Initial Entry Training - 19
- Technical Training or Additional Schools/Training - 27
- Duty Stations or Places of assignment (not including deployments) - 37
- Deployment - 53
- Combat - 79
- Funny, Unique and Bizarre Memories 92
- The Home Front - 97
- How I Was Affected - 103
- More Questions – 108
- Share Your Memories With Others - 119
- Resource Section – 120
    - Location of Your Military Records – 122
    - How to Get Replacement Medals & Certificates – 124
    - Online Resources - 130

Basic Information Sheet

Name   Age When I Entered the Service

_____

High School Attended

_____

Address When I Entered the Service

_____

_____

People I Lived With at the Time

_____

_____

Drafted?   Yes   No   Enlistment Date

_____

Branch of Service

_____

Initial Military Occupation

_____

_____

Other Military Occupations

_____

_____

_____

Overseas Duty

_____

_____

Units of Assignment

_____

_____

Date of Discharge   Age at Discharge

_____

Rank When Discharged

_____

Place Where Discharged

_____

Military Promotions

A military promotion is a significant achievement in a service member's career. It's a testament to their commitment, mastery of duties and skills, and to the service member's leadership capabilities. Some promotions are more meaningful than others, especially as service members move up in rank.

Use this page to keep track of the rank that you earned and the date it was awarded.

Rank	Date

My Medals

Name of Medal

Date Awarded   Location

Reason for Award

Name of Medal

Date Awarded   Location

Reason for Award

Name of Medal

Date Awarded   Location

Reason for Award

Name of Medal

Date Awarded   Location

Reason for Award

My Medals

Name of Medal

Date Awarded   Location

Reason for Award

Name of Medal

Date Awarded   Location

Reason for Award

Name of Medal

Date Awarded   Location

Reason for Award

Name of Medal

Date Awarded   Location

Reason for Award

My Medals

Name of Medal

Date Awarded   Location

Reason for Award

Name of Medal

Date Awarded   Location

Reason for Award

Name of Medal

Date Awarded   Location

Reason for Award

Name of Medal

Date Awarded   Location

Reason for Award

Other Recognitions

Type of Recognition

Date Awarded   Location

Reason for Award

Type of Recognition

Date Awarded   Location

Reason for Award

Type of Recognition

Date Awarded   Location

Reason for Award

Type of Recognition

Date Awarded   Location

Reason for Award

Military Friends

Use this page to keep track of the names and contact information for the military friends you keep in touch with

Name	Contact Information

Enlistment

This is the section to describe the things you remember about enlisting in the military. There is space to write about each of these prompts in the pages that follow. Remember, you don't have to answer every single question. Choose two or three that really get you thinking, and start writing! You can always add more later.

- Did you get into the branch of service that was your first choice or did you end up in another branch for some other reason?
- Were you drafted? If so, how did you feel about this?
- Where did you enlist, and on what date?
- Did your parents/family support you enlisting?
- Why did you enlist? For patriotism, for a job, to fight the enemy, or some other reason?
- Did the recruiters tell you the truth, or did they stretch it a bit to get you to sign up? (if you weren't drafted)
- Do you have memories of the enlistment physical or in-processing you endured?
- Did you leave for basic training immediately after enlisting, or was there time between enlistment and reporting for duty/service?

> "At my enlistment physical, they said I had too much wax in my left ear. They actually would not let me swear in to serve my country until it was cleaned out! So they put me into a taxi, dropped me off at a doctor's office and flushed my ear out. Once I returned to the MEPS (Military Entrance Processing Station) the doctor there checked my ear, and within minutes I was the newest member of the Ohio Army National Guard."
> -Claudia Bartow, Army and Air National Guards

Enlistment

Did you get into the branch of service that was your first choice or did you end up in another branch for some other reason?

_____
_____
_____
_____
_____
_____
_____
_____

Did your parents/family support you enlisting? Talk about the way you told them you were enlisting.

_____
_____
_____
_____
_____
_____
_____

Enlistment

Were you drafted? If so, how did you feel about this?

Where did you enlist, and on what date?

Enlistment

Why did you enlist? For patriotism, for a job, to fight the enemy, or some other reason?

_____
_____
_____
_____
_____
_____
_____
_____
_____
_____

Do you have memories of the enlistment physical or in-processing experience?

_____
_____
_____
_____
_____
_____
_____
_____
_____

Enlistment

Did the recruiters tell you the truth, or did they stretch it a bit to get you to sign up? (if you weren't drafted)

_____
_____
_____
_____
_____
_____
_____
_____

Was there time between enlistment and reporting for duty, or did you leave for basic right away? Why?

_____
_____
_____
_____
_____
_____
_____
_____

Boot Camp

Note: We realize different branches of service use different names for the initial training of their recruits. For some it is Basic Training, for others it's called Initial Entry Training. For simplicity's sake however, from here on, we will use the term "Boot Camp" to signify this training.

Some of the journal prompts that follow include:
- What happened when you arrived the very first time?
- Describe your first day at actual Boot Camp. Explain your feelings, the surroundings, and your most vivid memory.
- Who were your Drill Sergeants/Instructors? What were they like?
- What type of training did you do? Did you like it?
- What were the barracks (or where you stayed) like?
- Did you have certain duties you had to do? (KP, cleaning details, etc.)
- What was the food like? Give some examples of actual meals.

"We were in our 9th or 10th week of Basic Training and felt we were real Salts. Leaving the chow hall one afternoon six of us were marching back to our quarters. We passed a female Ensign who we, thinking it would be funny, gave a snappy left-handed salute. She immediately locked our heels, chewed us out, and then double-timed us back to our quarters where she turned us over to the company commander. Of course this was after she chewed him out for doing a bad job of training us in military etiquette. Needless to say life changed for us for the next couple of weeks."
-Bill McKinnon, U.S. Navy, Vietnam Era

Boot Camp

Location of Training

Dates of Training – from   to

How did you say goodbye to loved ones? Who was there to see you off?

Where was your boot camp located? What major city is this near? Did you spend much time there?

Boot Camp

What happened when you arrived the very first time?

_____
_____
_____
_____
_____
_____
_____
_____

Describe your first day at actual Boot Camp. Explain your feelings, the surroundings, and your most vivid memory.

_____
_____
_____
_____
_____
_____
_____
_____
_____
_____
_____

Boot Camp

Who were your Drill Sergeants/Instructors? What were they like?

_____
_____
_____
_____
_____
_____
_____
_____

What type of training did you do? Did you like it?

_____
_____
_____
_____
_____
_____
_____
_____

Boot Camp

Did you have certain duties you had to do? (KP, cleaning details, etc.)

_____
_____
_____
_____
_____
_____
_____
_____

What was the food like? Give some examples of actual meals.

_____
_____
_____
_____
_____
_____
_____
_____
_____

Boot Camp

What type of physical training did you do? Were there tests for this?

_____
_____
_____
_____
_____
_____
_____

What type of weapons did you learn to fire? Were you a good shot?

_____
_____
_____
_____
_____
_____
_____
_____

Boot Camp

What frustrated you the most about Boot Camp?

Who became your best friends in Boot Camp? Are you in contact with any of them today?

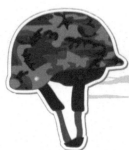

Boot Camp

What were the barracks like? Was it difficult sleeping in the same room with others?

_____
_____
_____
_____
_____
_____
_____

Did you go on leave after Boot Camp, (to where) or did you go straight to other training or deployment?

_____
_____
_____
_____
_____
_____
_____

Technical Schools

This section will vary from individual to individual due to personal experiences and different branches of service. There is space provided for three different schools or training. If you have additional schools or training, you can either copy blank pages and add more, or add these memories on the additional pages in the back of this journal. This could include training or schools you attended for promotion, for different military jobs, or for deployment/combat.

Some of the journal prompts for this section include:
- Who was in charge of you at this school or training? Describe them.
- Was the discipline strict or lax here? Explain.
- What type of training did you do? Did you like it?
- What did you struggle with? Where did you excel?
- How well did this school prepare you for what was to come?
- What are some funny things that happened to you or others?
- Where did you go after this training / school?

> I am a U.S. Navy Seabee — not too many people know who we are and what we do. We are known as the Navy's construction force. My particular "A" School was in Wichita Falls, Texas, at Sheppard Air Force Base. There for the first module, we learned how to troubleshoot heating, ventilation and air conditioning, learning the fundamentals of how heating, ventilation and air conditioning work. After that, we learned about plumbing. For me it was a really great learning experience, before I became a utilitiesman — I didn't even know that there were different types of plungers. I actually graduated at the top of my class.
>
> -Jessica Cruz San Roque, US Navy

27

Technical Schools

Name of School or Training

Location

Dates from   to

Purpose

Who was in charge of you at this school or training? Describe them.

What type of training did you do? Did you like it?

Technical Schools

What did you struggle with? Where did you excel?

_____
_____
_____
_____
_____
_____
_____
_____
_____

Was the discipling strict or lax there? Explain.

_____
_____
_____
_____
_____
_____
_____
_____

Technical Schools

How well did this training / school prepare you for what was to come? Give some examples.

Where did you go after this training/ school?

Technical Schools

Name of School or Training

Location

Dates from   to

Purpose

Who was in charge of you at this school or training? Describe them.

What type of training did you do? Did you like it?

Technical Schools

What did you struggle with? Where did you excel?

_____
_____
_____
_____
_____
_____
_____
_____
_____

Was the discipling strict or lax there? Explain.

_____
_____
_____
_____
_____
_____
_____
_____

Technical Schools

How well did this training / school prepare you for what was to come? Give some examples.

_____
_____
_____
_____
_____
_____
_____
_____

Where did you go after this training/ school?

_____
_____
_____
_____
_____
_____
_____
_____

Technical Schools

Name of School or Training

Location

Dates from   to

Purpose

Who was in charge of you at this school or training? Describe them.

What type of training did you do? Did you like it?

Technical Schools

What did you struggle with? Where did you excel?

Was the discipling strict or lax there? Explain.

Technical Schools

How well did this training / school prepare you for what was to come? Give some examples.

_____
_____
_____
_____
_____
_____
_____
_____

Where did you go after this training/ school?

_____
_____
_____
_____
_____
_____
_____
_____
_____

Duty Stations

For some of you, duty stations, deployment and combat may be the same thing. If that is the case, feel free to combine the answers for these sections as you see fit.

For this guide, "duty station" is defined as the home base/port/post. There is space for five duty stations. This is where you were when you weren't deployed on a mission.

Some of the journal prompts in this section include:
- Where was this duty station? What unit was this?
- What dates were you here?
- What was your job at this duty station? What did you do daily?
- What type of training was required at this place?
- What was this duty station famous for? (strict MPs, terrible food, etc.)
- Did you like it here? Why or why not?
- Where did you live? If you were single, were you in barracks, etc.?

In October 1965, 21-year-old Peter was drafted by the U.S. military during the height of the Vietnam War — he decided to join the Navy. Immediately after boot camp, Peter was stationed at Naval Degaussing Station in Charleston, SC., where he remained for the full two years. To this day, Peter is grateful for the camaraderie he built with his fellow base members, and the chance to earn his bachelor's degree before the end of his service.

-Peter, US Navy '65-'57

Duty Stations

Duty Station #1	Unit

Location
_____

Dates from _____ to _____

What was your job at this duty station? What did you do daily?

_____

_____

_____

_____

_____

_____

What type of training did you do? Did you like what you were being taught?

_____

_____

_____

_____

_____

_____

_____

_____

Duty Stations

| Duty Station #1 | Unit |

Did you like it there? Why or why not?

Where did you live? If you were single, were you in barracks, etc.?

Duty Stations

Duty Station #1	Unit

What was this duty station known for? (struck MP's, terrible food, etc.)
_____
_____
_____
_____
_____
_____
_____
_____

Did you get in any trouble while you were there?
_____
_____
_____
_____
_____
_____
_____
_____
_____

Duty Stations

Duty Station #2	Unit

Location

Dates from   to

What was your job at this duty station? What did you do daily?

_____
_____
_____
_____
_____
_____
_____

What type of training did you do? Did you like what you were being taught?

_____
_____
_____
_____
_____
_____
_____
_____

Duty Stations

| Duty Station #2 | Unit |

Did you like it there? Why or why not?

_____
_____
_____
_____
_____
_____
_____
_____

Where did you live? If you were single, were you in barracks, etc.?

_____
_____
_____
_____
_____
_____
_____
_____

Duty Stations

| Duty Station #2 | Unit |

What was this duty station known for? (struck MP's, terrible food, etc.)
_____
_____
_____
_____
_____
_____
_____
_____

Did you get in any trouble while you were there?
_____
_____
_____
_____
_____
_____
_____
_____
_____

Duty Stations

Duty Station #3	Unit

Location

Dates from to

What was your job at this duty station? What did you do daily?

_____
_____
_____
_____
_____
_____
_____

What type of training did you do? Did you like what you were being taught?

_____
_____
_____
_____
_____
_____
_____
_____

Duty Stations

| Duty Station #3 | Unit |

Did you like it there? Why or why not?
_____
_____
_____
_____
_____
_____
_____
_____

Where did you live? If you were single, were you in barracks, etc.?
_____
_____
_____
_____
_____
_____
_____
_____

Duty Stations

Duty Station #3	Unit

What was this duty station known for? (struck MP's, terrible food, etc.)
___
___
___
___
___
___
___
___

Did you get in any trouble while you were there?

___
___
___
___
___
___
___
___
___

Duty Stations

Duty Station #4	Unit

Location

Dates from	to

What was your job at this duty station? What did you do daily?

_____
_____
_____
_____
_____
_____

What type of training did you do? Did you like what you were being taught?

_____
_____
_____
_____
_____
_____
_____
_____

Duty Stations

Duty Station #4	Unit

Did you like it there? Why or why not?
_____
_____
_____
_____
_____
_____
_____
_____
_____
_____

Where did you live? If you were single, were you in barracks, etc.?
_____
_____
_____
_____
_____
_____
_____
_____
_____

Duty Stations

| Duty Station #4 | Unit |

What was this duty station known for? (struck MP's, terrible food, etc.)

_____
_____
_____
_____
_____
_____
_____
_____

Did you get in any trouble while you were there?

_____
_____
_____
_____
_____
_____
_____
_____
_____
_____

Duty Stations

Duty Station #5	Unit

Location

Dates from   to

What was your job at this duty station? What did you do daily?

_____
_____
_____
_____
_____
_____

What type of training did you do? Did you like what you were being taught?

_____
_____
_____
_____
_____
_____
_____
_____

Duty Stations

Duty Station #5	Unit

Did you like it there? Why or why not?
_____
_____
_____
_____
_____
_____
_____
_____

Where did you live? If you were single, were you in barracks, etc.?
_____
_____
_____
_____
_____
_____
_____
_____

Duty Stations

Duty Station #5	Unit

What was this duty station known for? (struck MP's, terrible food, etc.)
_____
_____
_____
_____
_____
_____
_____
_____

Did you get in any trouble while you were there?
_____
_____
_____
_____
_____
_____
_____
_____
_____

Deployment

For some veterans, deployment and combat are the same. Feel free to combine the answers to these deployment and the combat questions if you would like.

For this journal deployment is defined as follows:
You have a set of orders to go to a place, usually overseas, to perform a mission during wartime. This would include cruises in the Navy or Coast Guard.

While actual combat may not have happened directly to you, you are supporting the overall military mission. This of course includes National Guard and Reserve units. There is room in this journal to note your reflections about five separate deployment times.

Some journal prompts in this section include:
- How did you learn your unit was going to be deployed?
- How did you feel about this?
- How did this affect your loved ones and your relationship with them?
- What unit/ship were you assigned to? How many people deployed?
- What was your rank and military job at the time?
- What type of training did do to prepare for deployment? Where was this done? What was it like?

> In 2004, I had orders to be stationed on the U.S.S. Fitzgerald, which at the time was stationed in San Diego. When my ship finally pulled in, I found out I was the first female enlisted sailor to ever be stationed onboard. They didn't even have a place for me to sleep.
>
> -Jean Coriat,
> Petty Officer First Class, Retired, Navy 2004-18

Deployment

Dates from							to

Unit of assignment					How many people deployed?

Deployed to

What was your rank and military job at the time?

How did you learn your unit was going to be deployed?

How did you feel about this?

54

Deployment

How did this affect your loved ones and your relationship with them?

_____
_____
_____
_____
_____
_____
_____
_____

What type of training did you do to prepare for deployment? Where was this done? What was it like?

_____
_____
_____
_____
_____
_____
_____
_____
_____
_____
_____
_____

Deployment

What transportation was used to get you to your final deployment destination?

_____
_____
_____
_____
_____
_____
_____
_____
_____
_____

What was your unit's mission on this deployment?

_____
_____
_____
_____
_____
_____
_____
_____
_____
_____
_____

Deployment

What was your daily life like on this deployment?

Describe your homecoming experience. Who was there?

Deployment

Other thoughts about this time

Deployment

Dates from _____ to _____

Unit of assignment _____ How many people deployed? _____

Deployed to _____

What was your rank and military job at the time?

How did you learn your unit was going to be deployed?

How did you feel about this?

Deployment

How did this affect your loved ones and your relationship with them?

_____
_____
_____
_____
_____
_____
_____
_____

What type of training did you do to prepare for deployment? Where was this done? What was it like?

_____
_____
_____
_____
_____
_____
_____
_____
_____
_____
_____

Deployment

What transportation was used to get you to your final deployment destination?

What was your unit's mission on this deployment?

Deployment

What was your daily life like on this deployment?

_____
_____
_____
_____
_____
_____
_____
_____
_____

Describe your homecoming experience. Who was there?

_____
_____
_____
_____
_____
_____
_____
_____
_____
_____

Deployment

Other thoughts about this time

Deployment

Dates from   to

Unit of assignment   How many people deployed?

Deployed to

What was your rank and military job at the time?

How did you learn your unit was going to be deployed?

How did you feel about this?

Deployment

How did this affect your loved ones and your relationship with them?

_____
_____
_____
_____
_____
_____
_____
_____

What type of training did you do to prepare for deployment? Where was this done? What was it like?

_____
_____
_____
_____
_____
_____
_____
_____
_____

Deployment

What transportation was used to get you to your final deployment destination?

_____
_____
_____
_____
_____
_____
_____
_____
_____

What was your unit's mission on this deployment?

_____
_____
_____
_____
_____
_____
_____
_____
_____
_____
_____

Deployment

What was your daily life like on this deployment?

_____
_____
_____
_____
_____
_____
_____
_____
_____
_____

Describe your homecoming experience. Who was there?

_____
_____
_____
_____
_____
_____
_____
_____
_____
_____

Deployment

Other thoughts about this time

Deployment

Dates from   to

Unit of assignment   How many people deployed?

Deployed to

What was your rank and military job at the time?

How did you learn your unit was going to be deployed?

How did you feel about this?

Deployment

How did this affect your loved ones and your relationship with them?

What type of training did you do to prepare for deployment? Where was this done? What was it like?

Deployment

What transportation was used to get you to your final deployment destination?

What was your unit's mission on this deployment?

Deployment

What was your daily life like on this deployment?

_____
_____
_____
_____
_____
_____
_____
_____
_____
_____

Describe your homecoming experience. Who was there?

_____
_____
_____
_____
_____
_____
_____
_____
_____
_____

Deployment

Other thoughts about this time

Deployment

Dates from _____ to _____

Unit of assignment _____ How many people deployed? _____

Deployed to _____

What was your rank and military job at the time?

_____
_____

How did you learn your unit was going to be deployed?

_____
_____
_____
_____
_____
_____
_____

How did you feel about this?

_____
_____
_____
_____
_____

Deployment

How did this affect your loved ones and your relationship with them?

_____
_____
_____
_____
_____
_____
_____
_____

What type of training did you do to prepare for deployment? Where was this done? What was it like?

_____
_____
_____
_____
_____
_____
_____
_____
_____
_____

Deployment

What transportation was used to get you to your final deployment destination?

_____
_____
_____
_____
_____
_____
_____
_____

What was your unit's mission on this deployment?

_____
_____
_____
_____
_____
_____
_____
_____
_____

Deployment

What was your daily life like on this deployment?

Describe your homecoming experience. Who was there?

Deployment

Other thoughts about this time

Combat

If you have experienced combat, this is where you can talk about it. There is space for three combat actions. Additional blank pages in the back of this guide can be used to record additional experiences. You could also use these sections for individual battles or engagements. It is your decision as to how much detail you share here.

This section of the journal is not intended to upset you or bring up bad memories. For some, writing about these experiences is helpful, for others it is not. If it is the latter, please skip this section. Maybe at some other time it will be useful for you.

God Bless those of you who had no real homecoming, or a negative experience, especially from the Korean and Vietnam Wars. Welcome Home! And thank you for your service.

> I do not have PTSD, but if I watch part of a movie like 'The Hurt Locker,' or when I spend time around Blackhawk helicopters, I will close my eyes that night and live an entire day in Iraq, flying my missions. I remember the smell and the feel and the heat and everything about it. Then I wake up in Illinois, and I'm exhausted.
> **Tammy Duckworth**

Combat

Dates of combat action from   to

Unit or ship assignment

Location of combat

My personal job

What was your mission or objective?

What was a typical day like for you during combat?

What type of weapon(s) did you carry or fire?

Combat

What were the living conditions like? The food? Any sleep?

_____
_____
_____
_____
_____
_____
_____
_____

Describe your scariest moment.

_____
_____
_____
_____
_____
_____
_____
_____
_____
_____
_____

Combat

Did you or someone you know commit great acts of bravery? Tell about it.

_____
_____
_____
_____
_____
_____
_____

Were you ever injured? How did you recover?

_____
_____
_____
_____
_____
_____
_____
_____
_____
_____

Combat

Did you lose any of your friends? Memorialize them here.

_____
_____
_____
_____
_____
_____
_____
_____
_____
_____

Describe your homecoming.

_____
_____
_____
_____
_____
_____
_____
_____

Combat

Dates of combat action from   to

Unit or ship assignment
_____

Location of combat

My personal job
_____

What was your mission or objective?
_____

What was a typical day like for you during combat?
_____
_____
_____
_____
_____

What type of weapon(s) did you carry or fire?
_____
_____

Combat

What were the living conditions like? The food? Any sleep?

_____
_____
_____
_____
_____
_____
_____
_____
_____

Describe your scariest moment.

_____
_____
_____
_____
_____
_____
_____
_____
_____
_____
_____

Combat

Did you or someone you know commit great acts of bravery? Tell about it.

Were you ever injured? How did you recover?

Combat

Did you lose any of your friends? Memorialize them here.

Describe your homecoming.

Combat

Dates of combat action from _____ to _____

Unit or ship assignment
_____

Location of combat
_____

My personal job
_____
_____

What was your mission or objective?
_____
_____

What was a typical day like for you during combat?
_____
_____
_____
_____
_____
_____
_____

What type of weapon(s) did you carry or fire?
_____
_____
_____

Combat

What were the living conditions like? The food? Any sleep?

Describe your scariest moment.

Combat

Did you or someone you know commit great acts of bravery? Tell about it.

_____
_____
_____
_____
_____
_____
_____
_____

Were you ever injured? How did you recover?

_____
_____
_____
_____
_____
_____
_____
_____
_____

Combat

Did you lose any of your friends? Memorialize them here.

Describe your homecoming.

Funny, Unique & Bizarre

Military service seems to be synonymous with funny, unique and bizarre situations, coincidences and stories. Thus, it gets its own section!

We've provided plenty of room to write your thoughts. You may have one bizarre story or four. Just skip a line, give your recollection or story a title, and write it down.

This will probably end up being one of your favorite sections, and your loved ones will certainly enjoy it as well.

> I was a civilian working on a military base. My manager was military and had been sent on a course to qualify to get a promotion. She came back and was not herself. She was quiet and seemed sad.
>
> At lunch, she told my coworkers and me why she was sad. It had turned out that she was not allowed to yell at the civilians. Even if we made errors and even — and for her this was obviously the worst part — if she had slept badly or just needed to express that she was in a bad mood.

Funny, Unique & Bizarre

Bad food or meal

_____
_____
_____
_____
_____
_____
_____

Crazy / funny / troublemaker people who trained with you

_____
_____
_____
_____
_____
_____
_____
_____
_____
_____
_____
_____

Funny, Unique & Bizarre

Crazy/funny/super-strict Drill Sergeants or Commanding Officers or Non-Commissioned Officers

A coincidence to top all coincidences

Funny, Unique & Bizarre

Times when "hurry up and wait" truly deserved the title

_____
_____
_____
_____
_____
_____
_____
_____
_____
_____
_____
_____

Talk about meeting or seeing a famous person while in the service

_____
_____
_____
_____
_____
_____
_____
_____
_____
_____
_____
_____

Funny, Unique & Bizarre

Did you experience a close call? Tell the situation.

Crazy or unseasonable weather stories

The Home Front

This section is dedicated to your loved ones back home. Only you and they know the true sacrifice endured while you were away during military service, whether it was at training, deployments or in combat.

Use this area as a place for loved ones can write, if they so desire. We highly encourage you to place copies of letters, postcards or emails with a hard copy of your responses for future reference. Blank pages have been provided.

Feel free to include more information about a homecoming in this section.

> "I remember getting off the bus from Iraq and seeing my dad standing there with tears in his eyes. I had only seen my father cry one time and that was when grandpa died. It was a special moment for me and one that I will never forget. My dad is a Vietnam Vet and had not talked with me about that war and what he went thru until I came home. I could see the pride and happiness in dad's face."
>
> -Jerry Wheeler, U.S. Army, Iraqi War

The Home Front

Who did you communicate with when you were in training, at a duty station or on deployment?

_____
_____
_____

How did you communicate? V-mail, (during World War II) handwritten censored letters, e-mail, Skype, phone? Was it hard to receive word from home?

_____
_____
_____
_____
_____

How often did you get to communicate with folks back home?

_____
_____
_____

What was the impact on you when YOU received a letter, e-mail, package, etc?

_____
_____
_____
_____
_____

The Home Front

Did you have a girlfriend/boyfriend when you were away? A wife or husband?

_____
_____
_____
_____
_____
_____

Did you get married while you were in the service? Where and how did this happen?

_____
_____
_____
_____
_____
_____

What did it mean to have support from loved ones?

_____
_____
_____
_____
_____
_____

The Home Front

My Homecoming

The Home Front

Memories of Home

The Home Front

Memories of Home

_____
_____
_____
_____
_____
_____
_____
_____
_____
_____
_____
_____
_____
_____
_____
_____
_____
_____
_____

How I Was Affected

> Do you still...
> Make your bed with hospital corners?
> Square off a corner when you walk?
> Stand at attention for the National Anthem?

How Did Military Service Affect Your Life?

Whether you had a positive or negative experience in the military, it made an impact on your life. You may not realize the many small ways your life would be different if you had not worn the uniform.

Look through the prompt questions and use the blank pages to record your memories.

> It's not that people weren't friendly, and it's not that I didn't make friends. But it was never the same as it was in the military. In the military, the people you live with or near are also in the military. You're brought into the social life in ways you never are in civilian life."
>
> -Thomas Murrell, U.S. Air Force, Vietnam

How I Was Affected

Questions to think about:

- ❑ Are you always on time (or early) because of what you learned in the military?
- ❑ Do you wear or take care of your clothing in a certain way?
- ❑ Are there certain foods you grew to love (or hate) in the military and that feeling still persists today?
- ❑ Did you get your work ethic or style from the military?
- ❑ What job skills- technical or general- did you learn that you use in your civilian job or daily life?
- ❑ What habits did you learn that you still use today?
- ❑ Are there particular phrases, words or military lingo you use in your civilian life?
- ❑ Does it bother you when civilians do or say things that are not "military"?
- ❑ Are you more patriotic than before your service?
- ❑ Is your view of politics or news different because of it?

Share Your Memories – How have you changed?

_____
_____
_____
_____
_____
_____
_____

Share Your Memories – How have you changed?

Share Your Memories – How have you changed?

Share Your Memories – How have you changed?

More Questions

We hope you are enjoying sharing your memories with family and friends and have included several other journal prompts to continue the journey of recording your military service.

Your memories are important! They help us all to remember that your sacrifice is what makes our freedom possible.

If you do not have anything else to say, use this space to add photos of your time in service and of family and friends while you were deployed.

- Were there any other friends or family that enlisted at the same time you did?
- Do you have memories of your enlistment paperwork? Easy or hard to complete?
- Do you have memories of the enlistment physical or in-processing?
- What transportation did you use to get to boot camp?
- Was there some type of reception station where you received shots, did paperwork, went through classes? Describe this
- Did friends you made at Boot Camp stay with you at other training or deployments?
- Did you have family with you during your Duty Station time? If you had children, what school did they attend? Did they fit in?
- Who were your friends and neighbors at each Duty Station?
- Was there a send-off ceremony for your deployment? Where was it done? What was it like?
- Talk more about your injuries. Do they still affect you today?
- Share some liberty or leave stories that were memorable.
- Was there ever a time when there was humor during combat?
- Were you a prisoner of war? Tell me about your experiences in captivity and when freed.
- Did you have any extra duties during your time in service? This could be anything from latrine duty, to ammo detail, or training new troops.
- What are some fun things you and your friends did together while you were deployed?
- What phrase or word will never be the same now that you served?
- Was there something special you did for "good luck"?
- How did people entertain themselves? Were there entertainers?
- Do you have photographs? Tell about the people in the photographs.
- Did you keep a personal diary?
- When you were first discharged, what are some things about civilians that were difficult for you to deal with?
- Is there anything you wish civilians understood about military service?
- What are some things you miss about being in the service? What are some you are glad to have left behind?
- What has been difficult to communicate to family and friends about your military service?
- Have you joined a veterans organization? Why or why not.
- What did you go on to do as a career after the war?
- Have you had and did you attend any reunions?

115

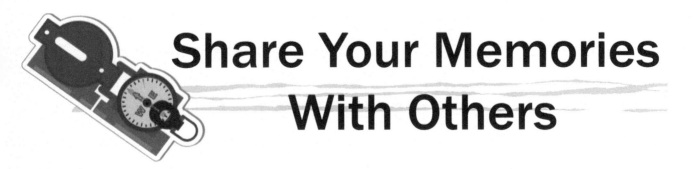

Share Your Memories With Others

Where and how you can share your memories

Congratulations! If you have gotten to this point of the guide, you have probably at least reminisced about your time in the military. Hopefully, you have put pen to paper, fingers on the keyboard, or even told some stories to a loved one.

You have these great memories and stories. So how else can you share them other than with your loved ones? We have compiled several ways you can contribute your memories. Some ways would happen in person, others online, still other places would like you to tape recorder your service history. We encourage you to be proud of whatever service you did, and share it for posterity.

Ideas of where and how to share:

Local schools

Did you know in many states it is a law that schools spend at least one hour during the school year recognizing veterans? Schools usually are happy to fulfill this requirement, and most do it on or near Veterans Day.

Call or email the Social Studies teacher at your local school. Explain to them you have recorded your memories of military service and would like to share them with the students. Most teachers will jump at the chance for you to visit, or at least take a copy of your memories for permanent placement in the school's library.

In early October call your local school and inquire about any Veterans' Day assemblies they might be having in the next month. There is a very good chance they are looking for veterans to attend and share, and may even ask you to speak.

Local colleges

More and more colleges are making efforts to collect veterans' stories. The best thing to do is call the Social Sciences Department of your local college and ask if there is a current project you can participate in.

Museums

Many military museums are looking for veterans' stories, memories, photos and memorabilia. Some would like your written stories; others would like audio or video versions of your service. If you have a museum in your city, county, or state, call them and ask how you can share.

> For a long time I didn't understand my father. He always seemed a little different from most of the other fathers I knew.
>
> My father spent over two years in Camp 1, Camp 4, and Camp 5 during the Korean War. His life long dream has been to have his story and the story of his buddies in the various POW Camps published.
>
> I am very glad to find that other sons and daughters have those feelings as well. It tells me that the men and women who became America's POWs and MIAs will truly not be forgotten, at least by my generation.
>
> -George J. Mata Jr.

Veterans Organizations

Groups like the American Legion, Veterans of Foreign Wars (VFWs), and American Veterans (AMVETS) are natural places to share your memories. You can be a member and share in person, or many Posts/Chapters have programs to collect veterans' histories.

These groups also need speakers from time to time and are serious about promoting involvement of veterans within schools and the community. The resources section in the back of this guide has the contact information for all major veterans' organizations

Civic organizations

Groups such as 4-H clubs, Boy Scout and Girl Scout units, Rotary, Kiwanis, public libraries, and local historical societies are always looking for unique projects and topics.

Veterans History Project

This is a huge effort by the Library of Congress. Its goal is as follows, "The Veterans History Project of the American Folklife Center collects, preserves, and makes accessible the personal accounts of American war veterans so that future generations may hear directly from veterans and better understand the realities of war."

The project collects first-hand accounts of U.S. Veterans from the following wars:

- World War, 1914-1918
- World War, 1939-1945
- Cold War
- Korean War, 1950-1953
- Vietnam War, 1961-1975
- Grenada--History--American Invasion, 1983
- Panama--History--American Invasion, 1989
- Operation Restore Hope, 1992-1993
- Persian Gulf War, 1991
- United Nations Operation in Somalia
- Haiti--History--American intervention, 1994-1995
- Operation Allied Force, 1999
- Peacekeeping forces--Bosnia and Hercegovina
- Operation Joint Guardian, 1999-
- War on Terrorism, 2001-2009
- Afghan War, 2001-
- Iraq War, 2003-2011

Find out more at https://www.loc.gov/vets/about.html

Resources

Information on service records, medals, benefits and useful links

How to Get Your Military Service Records

Your military service records are the key for you to receive the veterans' benefits you and your family are entitled to or qualify for, including medical care, pension, financial assistance and medals. Someday these records will be very important for the loved ones you leave behind for the purposes of funeral arrangements, possible benefits and genealogical research.

If you do not have a complete set of your military records, or you think there is an error, you can request copies of them from the National Personnel Records Center. Most veterans and their next of kin can receive free copies of the DD-214 paperwork.

The easiest way to obtain these records is on the National Personnel Records Center website at https://www.archives.gov/veterans/military-service-records . Follow their "Start Request Online" button to get step by step instructions to request your DD-214.

You also request this paperwork the old fashioned way. You can mail or fax your signed and dated request to the National Archives's National Personnel Record Center (NPRC). Most, but not all records, are stored at the NPRC. Be sure to use the address specified by eVetRecs if you do this online.

NPRC Mailing Address:
National Personnel Records Center
Military Personnel Records
1 Archives Drive
St. Louis, MO 63138
Phone 314-801-0800

NPRC Phone:
314-801-0800

NPRC Fax:
314-801-9195

Resources

Your request must contain certain basic information for them to locate your service records. This information includes:

- The veteran's complete name used while in service
- Service number
- Social security number
- Branch of service
- Dates of service
- Date and place of birth (especially if the service number is not known).

If you suspect your records may have been involved in the 1973 fire, also include:

- Place of discharge
- Last unit of assignment
- Place of entry into the service, if known.

All requests must be signed and dated by the veteran or next-of-kin. If you are the next of kin of a deceased veteran, you must provide proof of death of the veteran such as a copy of death certificate, letter from funeral home, or published obituary.

A note on response times from the Archives:

Allow about 10 days for us to receive and process your request, then you may check on the status. If you know your request number, click the red "Check Status" button on the https://www.archives.gov/veterans/military-service-records website. Requests that involve reconstruction efforts due to the 1973 Fire, or older records that require extensive search efforts, may take 6 months or more to complete. We work actively to respond to each request in a timely fashion, keep in mind we receive approximately 4,000 - 5,000 requests per day.

Please do not send a follow-up request before 90 days have elapsed, as it may cause further delays.

Resources

Location of Military Records

Wondering where the nation's millions of military records are kept?

If you've been discharged from military service, your personnel files are stored here at the National Archives and Records Administration (NARA). They are the official repository for records of military personnel who have been discharged from the U.S. Air Force, Army, Marine Corps, Navy and Coast Guard.

These charts from the federal government will help.

On July 12, 1973, a disastrous fire at the NPRC destroyed approximately 16-18 million Official Military Personnel Files. The records affected:

Branch	Personnel and Period Affected	Estimated Loss
Army	Personnel discharged November 1, 1912 to January 1, 1960	80%
Air Force	Personnel discharged September 25, 1947 to January 1, 1964 [with names alphabetically after Hubbard, James E	75%

Resources

Army (Includes Army Air Corps and Army Air Forces)

Dates of Service	Rank	Personnel Record Location	Health Record Location
1789 to November 1, 1912	Enlisted	NARA, Washington DC	N/A
1789 to July 1, 1917	Officer	NARA, Washington DC	N/A
November 1, 1912 to October 15, 1992 **Note:** Many records were destroyed by the 1973 Fire	Enlisted	National Personnel Records Center **Note:** Personnel records are Archival *62 years* after the service member's separation.	
July 1, 1917 to October 15, 1992 **Note:** Many records were destroyed by the 1973 Fire	Officer	National Personnel Records Center **Note:** Personnel records are Archival *62 years* after the service member's separation.	
October 16, 1992 to September 30, 2002	All Personnel	National Personnel Records Center	Department of Veterans Affairs
Discharged, deceased or retired on or after October 1, 2002 to December 31, 2013	All Personnel	U.S. Army Human Resources Command **Note:** records are stored electronically at AHRC but requests are serviced by: National Personnel Records Center	Department of Veterans Affairs
Discharged, deceased or retired on or after January 1, 2014	All Personnel	U.S. Army Human Resources Command **Note:** records are stored electronically at AHRC but requests are serviced by: National Personnel Records Center	AMEDD Record Processing Center
All active duty, including active Army Reserve	All Personnel	U.S. Army Human Resources Command	
All active and non-active duty National Guard	All Personnel	The Adjutant General (of the appropriate state, DC, or Puerto Rico)	

125

Resources

Air Force

Dates of Service	Rank	Personnel Record Location	Health Record Location
September 24, 1947 to May 1, 1994 **Note:** Many records were destroyed by the 1973 Fire	All Personnel	National Personnel Records Center **Note:** Personnel records are Archival 62 years after the service member's separation.	
May 1, 1994 to September 30, 2004	All Personnel	National Personnel Records Center	Department of Veterans Affairs
Discharged, deceased or retired from active duty on or after October 1, 2004 to December 31, 2013	All Personnel	Air Force Personnel Center HQ AFPC/DPSSRP	Department of Veterans Affairs
Discharged, deceased or retired from active duty on or after January 1, 2014	All Personnel	Air Force Personnel Center HQ AFPC/DPSSRP	AF STR Processing Center
Active (including National Guard on active duty in the Air Force), TDRL, or general officers retired with pay	All Personnel	Air Force Personnel Center HQ AFPC/DPSSRP	
Reserve, retired reserve in non-pay status, current National Guard officers not on active duty in the Air Force, or National Guard released from active duty in the Air Force	Various Personnel	Air Reserve Personnel Center HQ ARPC/DPTOCW (Contact Center)	
Current National Guard enlisted not on active duty in the Air Force	All Personnel	The Adjutant General (of the appropriate state, DC, or Puerto Rico)	

Resources

Navy

Dates of Service	Rank	Personnel Record Location	Health Record Location
1798 to 1885	Enlisted	NARA, Washington DC	N/A
1798 to 1902	Officer	NARA, Washington DC	N/A
1885 to January 30, 1994	Enlisted	National Personnel Records Center **Note:** Personnel records are Archival *62 years* after the service member's separation	
1902 to January 30, 1994	Officer	National Personnel Records Center **Note:** Personnel records are Archival *62 years* after the service member's separation	
January 31, 1994 to December 31, 1994	All Personnel	National Personnel Records Center	Department of Veterans Affairs
Discharged, deceased or retired on or after January 1, 1995 to December 31, 2013	All Personnel	Navy Personnel Command	Department of Veterans Affairs
Discharged, deceased or retired on or after January 1, 2014	All Personnel	National Personnel Records Center	BUMED Navy Medicine Records Activity

Resources

Marine Corps

Dates of Service	Rank	Personnel Record Location	Health Record Location
1798 to 1904	All Personnel	NARA, Washington DC	N/A
1905 to April 30, 1994	All Personnel	National Personnel Records Center **Note:** Personnel records are Archival *62 years* after the service member's separation	
May 1, 1994 to December 31, 1998	All Personnel	National Personnel Records Center	Department of Veterans Affairs
Discharged, deceased or retired on or after January 1, 1999 to December 31, 2013	All Personnel	U.S. Marine Corps, Manpower Management Records & Performance Branch (MMRP)	Department of Veterans Affairs
Discharged, deceased or retired on or after January 1, 2014	All Personnel	U.S. Marine Corps, Manpower Management Records & Performance Branch (MMRP)	BUMED Navy Medicine Records Activity
Individual Ready Reserve	All Personnel	Marine Forces Reserve	
Active, Selected Marine Corps Reserve, TDRL	All Personnel	U.S. Marine Corps, Manpower Management Records & Performance Branch (MMRP)	

Resources

Coast Guard [including Revenue Cutter Svc, Life-Saving Svc, Lighthouse Service

Dates of Service	Rank	Personnel Record Location	Health Record Location
Discharged, deceased or retired prior to December 31, 1897	All Personnel	NARA, Washington DC	N/A
January 1, 1898 to March 31, 1998	All Personnel	National Personnel Records Center **Note:** Personnel records are Archival *62 years* after the service member's separation	
Discharged, deceased or retired from active duty from April 1, 1998 to September 30, 2014	All Personnel	National Personnel Records Center	Department of Veterans Affairs
Discharged, deceased or retired from active duty on or after October 1, 2014	All Personnel	National Personnel Records Center	
Active, Reserve or TDRL	All Personnel	USCG Personnel Command	

Resources

Information on service records, medals, benefits and useful links

Medals, Ribbons, and Awards

https://www.archives.gov/veterans/replace-medals

If you served in any branch of service for any length of time, you are entitled to certain medals and their accompanying ribbons. Be proud of what you earned!

You should have been issued the medals and associated ribbons from your particular branch of service. However, many veterans either never receive these awards that are clearly stated on the discharge paperwork, or lose them over time.

If your discharge paperwork states you are entitled to a certain award and you need or want it, you can receive one free set from the government. A word to the wise, however, this is the government we're talking about so it does take a long time! Here is the process to receive what you (or your family members) earned:

For the Veteran: in general, the military services will work replacement medal requests for the veteran at no cost. This includes family members with the signed authorization of the veteran. https://www.archives.gov/personnel-records-center/sample-authorization

For the Next-of-Kin: the process (and cost) for replacement medals requests differs among the service branches and is dependent upon who is requesting the medal, particularly if the request involves an archival record.

Resources

Information on service records, medals, benefits and useful links

Medals, Ribbons, and Awards

https://www.archives.gov/veterans/replace-medals

For the General Public: if the service member separated from military service before 1960, the public may purchase a copy of the veteran's Official Military Personnel File (OMPF) to determine the awards due and obtain the medals from a commercial source. If the service member separated after 1960, the public may request such information from the OMPF via the Freedom of Information Act. https://www.archives.gov/personnel-records-center/ompf-access-public

Each branch of service is a little different in how they handle this process. The information below is from www.archives.gov.

If you already know which medals, ribbons, or awards you are entitled to, there is a way to get them much faster.

Check out this terrific source for medals, ribbons, awards, patches, and coins and much more at Medals of America 1-864-862-0635 or online at https://medalsofamerica.com

Not only do they stock everything you could possibly need, they are staffed with veterans who are experts in preparing ribbon racks and display cases.

Resources

Who is the Next-of-Kin (NOK)?

For the **Air Force, Navy, Marine Corps & Coast Guard**, the NOK is defined as: *the unremarried widow or widower, son, daughter, father, mother, brother or sister*

For the **Army**, the NOK is defined as: *the surviving spouse, eldest child, father or mother, eldest sibling or eldest grandchild*

If you do not meet the definition of NOK, you are considered a member of the general public.

Replace Your ARMY Medals

Where to write for medals	National Personnel Records Center 1 Archives Drive St. Louis, MO 63138 or https://www.archives.gov/veterans/military-service-records
Where medals are mailed from	U.S. Army TACOM Clothing and Heraldry (PSID) P.O. Box 57997 Philadelphia, PA 19111-7997
Where to write in case of a problem or an appeal	U.S. Army Human Resources Command Soldier Program and Services Division - Awards and Decorations Branch ATTN: AHRC-PDP-A 1600 Spearhead Division Avenue, Dept 480 Fort Knox, KY 40122-5408

Resources

Replace Your AIRFORCE Medals
(includes Army Air Corps & Mary Air Forces)

Where to write for medals	National Personnel Records Center 1 Archives Drive St. Louis, MO 63138 or https://www.archives.gov/veterans/military-service-records

	Active Duty Veterans	Reserve & Air Guard Veterans
Where medals are mailed from, and where to write in case of a problem or an appeal	Headquarters Air Force Personnel Center HQ AFPC/DP1SP 550 C Street West, Suite 12 Randolph AFB, TX 78150-4714	Air Reserve Personnel Center HQ ARPC/DPTARA 18420 E Silver Creek Ave Bldg 390 MS 68 Buckley AFB, CO 80011

Replace Your COASTGUARD Medals

Where to write for medals, and where medals are mailed from	Coast Guard Personnel Service Center 4200 Wilson Blvd, Suite 900 (PSC-PSD-MA) Stop 7200 Arlington, VA 20598-7200
Where to write in case of a problem or an appeal	Commandant U.S. Coast Guard Medals and Awards Branch (PMP-4) Washington, DC 20593-0001

Resources

Replace Your NAVY Medals

Where to write for medals	National Personnel Record Center 1 Archives Drive St. Louis, MO 63138 or https://www.archives.gov/veterans/military-service-records
Where medals are mailed from	Navy Personnel Command PERS 312 5751 Honor Drive Building 769 Room 158 Millington, TN 38055-3120
Where to write in case of a problem or an appeal	Department of the Navy Chief of Naval Operations (DNS-35) 2000 Navy Pentagon Washington, DC 20350-2000

Replace Your MARINE CORP Medals

Where to write for medals	National Personnel Record Center 1 Archives Drive St. Louis, MO 63138 or https://www.archives.gov/veterans/military-service-records
Where medals are mailed from	Navy Personnel Command PERS 312 5751 Honor Drive Building 769 Room 158 Millington, TN 38055-3120
Where to write in case of a problem or an appeal	Commandant of the Marine Corps Military Awards Branch (MMMA) 2008 Elliot Road Quantico, VA 22134

Online Resources

The granddaddy website when it comes to "all things military" is https://military.com Another useful site is https://vetfriends.com . It can help you track your military friends, as can using military.com's "Buddy Finder" and https://togetherweserved.com . Military.com also has a cool tool to find people who served in the same unit you did called the "Unit Finder."

Military Veterans Organizations

Below are links of military and veterans' organizations for just about any military subgroup or interest. Visit the website for more information.

Air Force Association   https://www.afa.org

Air Force Sergeants Association   https://www.hqafsa.org/

American Ex-Prisoners of War   https://www.axpow.org

American G.I. Forum   https://www.agif-nvop.org/

American Legion   https://www.legion.org

American Legion Riders   https://www.legion.org/riders

AMVETS (Amvets)   https://www.amvets.org

Blinded Veterans Association   https://www.bva.org

Catholic War Veterans & Auxiliary   https://wp2.cwv.org/

Cherokee Nation Warriors Society   https://veterans.cherokee.org

Combat Veterans Motorcycle Assoc   https://www.combatvet.us/

Disabled American Veterans (DAV)   https://www.dav.org

Dogs on Deployment   https://www.dogsondeployment.org/

Fallen Patriots [College for their children]   https://www.fallenpatriots.org/

Note: These sites were last accessed April 2021.

Online Resources

Freedom Remembered   https://freedomremembered.com

Fleet Reserve Association   https://www.fra.org

Great Americans- A Video Site   https://www.greatamericans.com/pages/military

Guardian Angels for Soldiers Pets   https://gafsp.org/

Iraq and Afghanistan Veterans of America   https://iava.org

Korean War Veterans Association   https://kwva.us

Marine Corps League   https://mcleague.com/

Military Officers Association of America   https://moaa.org

Military Order of the Purple Heart   https://purpleheart.org

Military Women's Memorial   https://womensmemorial.org/

National Coalition for Homeless Veterans   https://nchv.org

National Veteran-Owned Business Association   https://navoba.org

North Carolina Submarine Vets   https://ncsubvets.org/

PACT for Animals   https://pactforanimals.org/

Paralyzed Veterans of America   https://pva.org

Retired Enlisted Association (TREA)   https://trea.org

Salute America's Heroes   https://saluteheroes.org/

Sons of Union Veterans of the Civil War   http://www.suvcw.org/

Sons of Confederate Veterans   https://scv.org/

Student Veterans of America   https://studentveterans.org/

Union County Veterans Memorial   https://www.ucvetmemorial.org/

Veterans History Project @ the Library of Congress   https://www.loc.gov/vets/

Online Resources

Veterans of Foreign Wars   https://vfw.org/

Vietnam Veterans of America   https://vva.org/

Women Marines Association   https://www.womenmarines.org/

World War II- In Their Own Words   https://lmww2.com

Wounded Warrior Project   https://woundedwarriorproject.org

Military Aid Organizations and Other Useful Sites

This section features many wonderful organizations, which help military members, veterans and their families. Visit the website for more information.

Air Force Aid Society   https://afas.org/

American Red Cross   https://redcross.org

The Armed Forces Families Foundation   http://www.armedforcesfamilies.org/

Army Emergency Relief   https://www.armyemergencyrelief.org/

Army MWR   https://www.armymwr.com/

Coast Guard Mutual Assistance   https://cgmahq.org/

Fallen Patriot Fund   https://fallenpatriotfund.org

Homefront Military Network   https://homefrontmilitarynetwork.org/

The Freedom Alliance   https://freedomalliance.org

Homes for Our Troops   https://www.hfotusa.org/

Military OneSource   https://militaryonesource.mil

National Assoc of Veterans & Families   https://www.navf.org/

Navy-Marine Corps Relief Society   https://nmcrs.org

Operation Hero Miles   https://fisherhouse.org/programs/hero-miles

Online Resources

US Army Warrant Officers Assoc.   https://usawoa.org

Operation Purple Camp https://militaryfamily.org/operation-purple/operation-purple-camp

Soldiers' Angels   https://soldiersangels.org

Together We Served   https://togetherweserved.com

The Tragedy Assistance Program for Survivors (TAPS)   https://www.taps.org/

Veterans Advantage   https://www.veteransadvantage.com/

Veterans of Foreign Wars   https://www.vfw.org

Yellow Ribbon America   https://wp.yellowribbonamerica.org

Want to send a care package to our troops? Here are some worthy organizations that will help you.

Adopt a Platoon   https://www.adoptaplatoon.org/

A Million Thanks   https://amillionthanks.org/

Any Soldier   http://anysoldier.com/

Army and Air Force Exchange Services   https://www.shopmyexchange.com/

Blue Star Mothers   https://www.bluestarmothers.org/

Books for Soldiers   https://booksforsoldiers.com/

Cell Phones for Soldiers   https://www.cellphonesforsoldiers.com/

Commissary Gift Certificates   https://www.commissaries.com/shopping/gift-cards

Operation Gratitude   https://www.operationgratitude.com/

Operation Homefront Hugs   https://www.homefronthugs.org/

Operation USO Care Package   https://www.uso.org/

If you know of a deserving website that should be on this list, or of any mistakes, please let us know and we will include it in the next update.